Giant George
and the Robin

Written by Jeanne Willis
Illustrated by Barbara Vagnozzi

Over the bridge, there is a village.
In the village, there is a lane.
The goblins call it Gypsy Lane.

In Gypsy Lane, there is a cottage.
It's a large cottage.
It's much too large for a goblin.

But the cottage is too small for a giant.
It's much too small for a giant like George.

Giant George is HUGE.
He's so huge, he cannot get out.
He's so huge, no one can get in.

Giant George is trapped.
Then he sees a jolly robin in the hedgerow.

"I wish I could change into a jolly robin," says Giant George. "I would fly away."

The robin hops on to the ledge.
Giant George scoops her up!

Giant George puts the robin in a cage.
It's much too small for a robin.

"Will you be my friend?" asks Giant George.
"If you set me free," says the robin,
"I'll be a friend to you."

"But how will you be my friend?" asks Giant George.
"Just set me free," says the robin, "and I'll show you."

Giant George lets the robin out.
She pecks him gently on the cheek.

How strange magic is!
Giant George's wish comes true.
He gets smaller and smaller until ...

... he changes into a robin!
He jumps out on to the hedge.
He is free!

Giant George flies away with his friend.
Over the hedgerow and over the cottage.

There they go!
Down Gypsy Lane.
Out of the village, over the bridge.
And up into the sky.